The Secret Message

One Friday afternoon,
Mrs. Martel said to her class,
"For the last half hour today,
I'm going to teach you how to
figure out a secret message."

And she showed the children a chart.

1	2	3	4	5	6	7	8	9	10	11	12	13
a	b	c	d	e	f	g	h	i	j	k	l	m

14	15	16	17	18	19	20	21	22	23	24	25	26
n	o	p	q	r	s	t	u	v	w	x	y	z

What were the children going to do
for the last half hour?

They were going to learn
how to figure out a secret message.

Holly said,
"You have put all the numbers from 1 to 26
on the chart, Mrs. Martel."

"And you have put the letters
of the alphabet under the numbers," said David.

"Yes," said Mrs. Martel.
"Now, here is a page
of graph paper
for each of you."

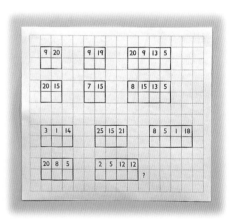

What had Mrs. Martel written
above each letter of the alphabet?

She had written the numbers 1 to 26.

"There are groups of numbers on our paper," said Angus.

"How do you think you could figure out a message in words from this code?" asked Mrs. Martel.

"I think I know what to do!" said Holly, looking up at the chart. "We have to write down the letter for each number."

"The first two numbers are 9 and 20," said Asha. "So the first word must be **it**."

What letters will Asha write under the 9 and the 20?

She will write the letter i under the number 9, and the letter t under the number 20.

"Well done, Holly and Asha," said Mrs. Martel.
"Now everyone knows what to do.
And when you have finished, just sit and wait.
When the time is right,
you will all say one word together.
This word will tell me
that you have figured out the message."

Angus said to his friend, Cameron,
"The second word has the number 9 in it, too.
And the letter for number 19 is **s**.
I know that this word says **is**."

What will the children do when they have finished figuring out the message?

They will sit and wait until **the time is right**.

"We have the third word," said Holly.
"We only had to look for two new letters.
Look! The third word is **time**."

"And I can see that the next three words
all have an **o** in them," said Asha.
"Let's fill in the rest of the letters!"

"I've got it!" said Cameron.
"The first sentence says, **It is time to go home**."

Angus looked at the clock.
"It's nearly time to go home," he said.
"The bell will be ringing in ten more minutes."

What is the last word in the sentence?

The last word in the sentence is **home**.

"We have another sentence to do yet," said Angus.
"The first word in it is **can**."

"The next word begins with a **y**," said Holly. "There are twenty-six letters in the alphabet, so number 25 will be the second to last letter. The word is **you**."

"I'll figure out the next word," said Asha. "**h... e... a... r**.   It's **hear**."

How many sentences are there in the message?

There are two sentences in the message.

"I've done the last two words,"
said Asha. "The message says,
**It is time to go home.
Can you hear the bell?"**

"Quick! Sit up!" said Holly.
"Everyone has finished."

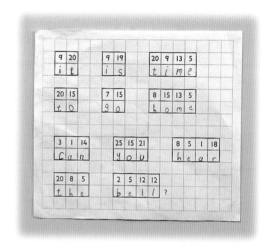

Just then the bell began to ring.
"**Yes!**" shouted the children,
and they all started to laugh.

"And now you can go home!" smiled Mrs. Martel.

What does this secret message say?

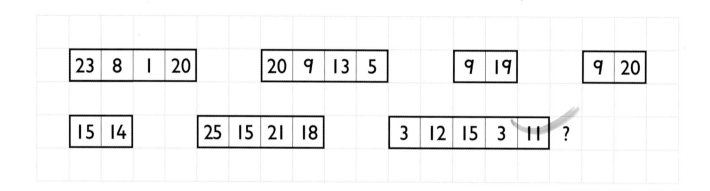

23	8	1	20

20	9	13	5

9	19

9	20

15	14

25	15	21	18

| 3 | 12 | 15 | 3 | 11 | ?
|---|----|----|---|----|

1	2	3	4	5	6	7	8	9	10	11	12	13
a	b	c	d	e	f	g	h	i	j	k	l	m

14	15	16	17	18	19	20	21	22	23	24	25	26
n	o	p	q	r	s	t	u	v	w	x	y	z